Alfred Williams Momerie

The Basis of Religion

being an examination of the more important arguments for and against

believing in that religion

Alfred Williams Momerie

The Basis of Religion
being an examination of the more important arguments for and against believing in that religion

ISBN/EAN: 9783337262761

Printed in Europe, USA, Canada, Australia, Japan

Cover: Foto ©Lupo / pixelio.de

More available books at **www.hansebooks.com**

THE BASIS OF RELIGION

BEING AN

EXAMINATION OF "NATURAL RELIGION"

BY THE

REV. A. W. MOMERIE, M.A., D.Sc.

FELLOW OF ST JOHN'S COLLEGE, CAMBRIDGE;
PROFESSOR OF LOGIC AND METAPHYSICS
IN KING'S COLLEGE, LONDON

WILLIAM BLACKWOOD AND SONS
EDINBURGH AND LONDON
MDCCCLXXXIII

PREFACE.

THE substance of the following Essay I delivered, as Select Preacher, before the University of Cambridge. As the sermon-form, however, was not necessary to the argument, and as many persons never read sermons *upon principle*, it appeared advisable to publish it in its present shape.

I should like to take this opportunity of saying that for the author of 'Ecce Homo' I shall always feel the deepest reverence and gratitude. I am not, of course, blind to the literary charm and other excellences of 'Natural Religion.' But in spite of its fascination, it appears to me exceedingly faulty in argument, and to some extent even pernicious in tendency. Pernicious for this reason : let us once be persuaded that the negative theories of modern science are compatible with religion, and we lose the strongest motive for that re-examination of the grounds on which the theories rest, which is the crying want of the present day. Whereas, on the contrary, if it be seen that these negative views divest the universe of all beauty, and make worship in this life and hope for the next utterly impossible, there will be less danger of their being accepted with undue haste and on insufficient evidence.

I should also like to take this opportunity of saying I cannot but feel very strongly that much time and scholarship and ability are being at present *wasted* by theologians. Work which is useful enough in one age becomes often perfectly futile in the next. Now modern science conceives that it has disproved the existence of the soul and of the Deity. Nothing can show that a Being, whom there is no reason to suppose existent (viz., God), has done anything to reveal Himself to another being, whom there is every reason to suppose non-existent (viz., the human soul). Of what use, then, to those who are imbued with the new ideas—and the number is increasing with tremendous rapidity—are treatises on the authorship of the Fourth Gospel, or on the credibility of miracles, or on minute points of Biblical exegesis ? Those who wish to do anything for the continuance of religion upon earth, should devote the best of their energies to the task of proving that our common experience, if we look deeply enough into it, contains super-sensible, and therefore supernatural elements— elements which may form a rational basis for a rational theology.

A. W. M.

KING'S COLLEGE, LONDON.

CONTENTS.

THE BASIS OF RELIGION.

INTRODUCTION.

The author of 'Ecce Homo' has been called, and I think justly, the interpreter of the age to itself. His writings, those at least which come from him in his prophetic or religious character, possess a peculiar solemnity and importance. No book, I believe, ever did so much as 'Ecce Homo' to broaden and deepen men's views of Christianity. A certain philanthropic but uncritical earl declared it at the time to be the vilest book ever vomited from the jaws of hell. It would be nearer the mark to call it the noblest book ever issued from the precincts of heaven. Thousands of men and women in the present day, I imagine, understand the Saviour better and love Him more because of what that book has taught them. The representation it offers of the life and work of Christ satisfies at once their reason

A

and their heart; it seems the very view towards which they had been unconsciously groping.

In 'Ecce Homo' the writer discussed Christianity mainly as it bore upon the present life. But he promised a second part, in which he would deal with it in its bearing upon a future state. Seventeen years passed by, however, and the second part was not forthcoming; when, just as we had begun to think he had withdrawn himself for ever from the region of theology, this new book was announced. One could guess from the title that this was not the promised second part of 'Ecce Homo,' but one could not guess what was the writer's precise object; and a great many persons seem to have been unable to divine his purpose even from a perusal of the book itself. Some of the reviewers gave us to understand that the author of 'Ecce Homo' had completely changed his views, that he had adopted the extremest scepticism of modern science, and that his last work was intended to justify his conversion to the ranks of materialism. Anything more absurd than this supposition could hardly be conceived, when it was made in the face of the following sentence, which occurs near the beginning of the first chapter :—

"Let us put religion by the side of science in its latest most aggressive form, with the view not of trying the question between them, but simply of measuring how much ground is common to both."

Since, however, this explicit statement had been misunderstood, he wrote a short preface to the second edition, in which he explained himself more fully as follows :—

" If it distresses any one to think that I personally abandon all that the extreme school call in question, certainly he may console himself. . . . In general the negative view is regarded in this book no otherwise than as I find it to be regarded by most of those to whom the book is principally addressed—viz., as a fashionable view difficult for the moment to resist, because it seems favoured by great authorities, a view therefore concerning which, however unwillingly, we cannot help asking ourselves the question, What if it should turn out to be true ? But if I were asked what I myself think of it, I should remark, that it is not the greatest scientific authorities who are so confident in negation, but rather the inferior men, who echo their opinions but who live themselves in the atmosphere not of science but of party controversy. . . .

" I find, however, that some readers have held that I must be taken to admit whatever in this book I do not undertake to refute, and have drawn the conclusion that I consciously reject Christianity ! Others have understood me to confess that on the questions at issue between religion and science I have nothing to say, a confession which I never meant to make. . . . I have always felt, and feel now as much as ever, that my views are Christian. I am surprised that any one can question it."

So much for our author's personal opinions. The real gist of his last book is this—It is engaged with the attempt to answer two questions : (1) Are the negative views of modern science compatible with any kind of religion ?

and (2) if so, what are the characteristics of that religion ?

A large number of eminent modern scientists reject, as every one knows, supernaturalism in all senses of the word. They not merely disbelieve in miracles, but they deny, or at any rate they say there is no reason for affirming, either the existence of God or the immortality of the soul. In fact, they maintain that the only soul we can know anything about is a soul indistinguishable and inseparable from brain. The word immortality is sufficient to sum up the differences between Christianity and this kind of negative science. The soul cannot be immortal if it be identical with a brain that is mortal: and again, if there be no immortality there is no God ; for the present world regarded as a system complete in itself is cruel and unjust. Conversely, if the soul be immortal, it must be a spiritual something separable from brain; and the discovery of such a non-material principle within ourselves is the first step towards the discovery of a God in Nature. So that, as I said, the word immortality may be taken as summing up the points at issue. The Christian believes in immortality; the modern negative scientist does not. In spite of this discrepancy, however, our author proposes to inquire whether there are not beliefs common to the two classes which can be properly called religious.

" It would certainly be hard enough to show that the present strife between Christianity and science is one in which insignificant differences are magnified by the imagination of the combatants. The question is nothing less than this, whether we are to regard the grave with assured hope, and the ties between human beings as indissoluble by death ; or, on the other hand, to dismiss the hope of a future life as too doubtful to be worth considering, even if not absolutely chimerical. No reasoning can make such a difference into a small one. But even where the differences are so great, it may still be worth while to call attention to the points of agreement. If there is some truth, however small, upon which all can agree, then there is some action upon which all can unite ; and who can tell how much may be done by anything so rare as absolute unanimity? Moreover, if we look below the surface of controversy, we shall commonly find more agreement and less disagreement than we had expected. Agreement is slow of speech and attracts little notice, disagreement has always plenty to say for itself. Agreement utters chiefly platitudes and truisms. And yet, though platitudes and truisms do not work up into interesting books, if our object is to accomplish something for human life, we shall scarcely find any truth serviceable that has not been rubbed into a truism, and scarcely any maxim that has not been worn into a platitude. Let the attempt then be made for once to apply this principle in the greatest and most radical of all controversies." [1]

In other words, let us inquire if there be such a thing as a purely natural religion,—a religion that does not involve any admixture of supernatural elements.

Now it is a very suggestive fact that this work

[1] P. 4.

upon 'Natural Religion' should have taken the place of 'Ecce Homo.' The "interpreter of the age to itself," instead of writing as he had promised, about the bearing of Christian theology on a future state, discusses the characteristics of a religion in which a future state is ignored. The growing prevalence of the negative views must have pressed very heavily on his heart. It has turned his thoughts—not his opinions; he distinctly tells us it has not changed them—but it has turned his thoughts into a totally new and unexpected channel. And there can be no doubt that the materialistic views are spreading far and fast. The few who take the lead in science, it is true, have not adopted them. Some years ago Mr Froude made the assertion that the foremost scientists had gone over in a body to the materialistic camp. But this was conclusively answered by Professor Tait, who mentioned the names of Brewster, Faraday, Forbes, Graham, Rowan, Hamilton, Herschel, Talbot—belonging to the immediate past; and Andrews, Joule, Clerk Maxwell, Balfour - Stewart, Stokes, and William Thomson—who were all at that time alive. "Surely," says Professor Tait, "there are no truly scientific thinkers in Britain more advanced than these; and each and all of them, when opportunity presented itself, have spoken in a sense altogether different from that implied by Mr Froude." The fact is, Mr Froude was probably thinking of men like the late Professor Clifford, Huxley, Bain, Herbert Spencer, Frederic Harrison, or John Morley. These are the men who instruct the masses. Owing to their popular style of writing or of lecturing, they enjoy a more extensive influence than others who rank higher as original investigators.

Now these men, though differing from one another in some important respects, are all more or less the apostles of negation. The late editor of the 'Fortnightly' feels certain that there is not, and cannot be, a God — so certain that he always writes the word with a little " g." Clifford, too, used to say he felt convinced, that if there were a God, the divine brain must long ago have been discovered in the course of our physical researches. Huxley and Spencer, on the other hand, so far from being dogmatic atheists, would be rather, according to our author, conspicuous examples of theists. They often speak eloquently of the great Power which is not ours, and they write it with a capital " P." Herbert Spencer in his 'First Principles' tries, like the author of the book we are examining, to bridge over the gulf between Religion and Science, and attempts to *prove* the existence of some Infinite Being, for whom he coins the name " Unknowable." Again, the popular writers and speakers, who, as I said, are the real teachers of the people, are not all professed materialists;

indeed many of them would be as much offended at being so called as they would at being designated spiritualists. But they all agree in two points—viz., in the denial of the soul and of God, in the common acceptation of those terms. They all agree in regarding consciousness as a mere function of brain. They all refuse to admit that our mental experience requires any non-material principle, such as we understand by the term soul or spirit.[1] They would all subscribe the dictum of Professor Bain, "the ego is a pure fiction coined from nonentity." In the opinion of all of them, therefore, immortality must be impossible; for if the soul be a pure fiction—a mere figment of the brain, it must dissolve with the brain's dissolution. These writers, therefore, are all at one in the denial of a separable soul. And secondly, we find the same unanimity among them in regard to the Christian conception of God. They all agree that the appearances of design in Nature do not imply any designing mind, but that they are sufficiently accounted for by the atomic theory and by natural selection. Further, they maintain that since consciousness, personality, and benevolence, are always in our experience connected with a nervous system, it is nothing less than gross

---

[1] In the 'First Principles,' Herbert Spencer might appear vaguely to admit some such entity, but in the 'Psychology' it is dogmatically denied.

anthropomorphism to attribute any such characteristics to the Power which is not ours. If we must call it God, we should remember it is an Unknown God. There is one thing, and one alone which we can discover about it—viz., that it is infinitely *stronger* than ourselves.

These are the opinions which, by means of reviews, pamphlets, text-books, and popular treatises, are being disseminated throughout the length and breadth of the land. They are becoming every day more popular, both among men of the highest culture at the universities, and also among men of no culture, such as your agnostic shoemakers and weavers. The other day we were informed in the newspapers that Mr Herbert Spencer was entertained at a banquet in New York. "There were over a hundred gentlemen present, comprising presidents of colleges, scientific men, authors, clergymen, and journalists of note." In the toast of the evening it was said to Mr Spencer, "we recognise in your knowledge greater comprehensiveness than in any other living man, or than has been presented by any one in our generation." There are hundreds and thousands in Great Britain to-day who would say the same. And the spread of agnostic philosophy, during the last fifty years, has been (to say the least) not less rapid on the Continent than in English-speaking countries. An enormous influence has been exercised by De Tracy,

Volney, Garat, Fourier, and Emile de Girardin, in France; and by Moleschott, Vogt, Büchner, and Haeckel in Germany.

The purpose of our author then, in ' Natural Religion,' would appear to be a highly laudable purpose. Since the negative views are spreading so quickly, and seem likely before long to be very generally adopted, it would, of course, console us, to find that even then things would not be so very bad, that even then men would still have a religion and a God. This is the task which our author has set himself. And if successfully accomplished, besides being a source of consolation, it might have been eminently serviceable in another and more important way. At present Christianity and science are regarded by the majority of partisans on both sides as absolutely antagonistic. And since science seems to be steadily gaining adherents and becoming stronger, and Christianity to be steadily losing adherents and becoming weaker, before long, it may be, science will assert itself and make a clean sweep of Christianity and indeed of all religion. Such a revolution, as our author justly observes, would endanger the very foundations of society. Instead, therefore, of this fierce conflict between religionists and scientists, there should be, he says, a grand coalition of all who are serious on both sides.[1]

[1] P. 232.

"Among men who profess alike to be materialists one is found excommunicating the other, shrinking from him with the horror of a Pharisee for a publican, and even pitying him with the pity of an apostle for a heathen. These feelings not only appear to have the nature of religion, but they are in no degree weak or faint. On the contrary they are fresh, and easily become violent. They by no means appear to be the mere survival of an extinct system of religion, but seem rather capable of becoming the germ of a new system."[1]

The scientists and the Christians who possess this spirit of earnestness should unite in a common crusade against their common enemies— against those, viz., who are destitute of earnestness; or, in other words, against what may be variously expressed as worldliness, secularity, conventionalism, Philistinism, stupidity, or selfishness. If the most negative of the scientists would only consider, they would find, he says, that they were in reality religious after all; that the root of the matter was in them; that though *in words* they refused to recognise a God, they did *in fact* acknowledge one, since they believed, and could not but believe, in something—call it nature, call it law, call it what you please—in obedience to whom alone could be found satisfaction and peace. The eternal law of the universe, he imagines, may become the basis of a new religion. It should form a bond of union between all earnest minds who recognise and

[1] P. 138.

obey it.   Since the scientific conception of law,
so far from being anti-Christian, is an essential
part of the Christian conception of the Deity,
scientists and Christians should join hands upon
it.   Christians, instead of anathematising men
of science, should recognise in them co-worship-
pers of God.   And scientists, instead of attempting to destroy Christianity and the Church, should
adopt the existing ecclesiastical organisation, re-
vivify it with their own scientific enthusiasm,
and use it as an instrument for missionary en-
terprise at home and abroad—as an instrument
for the steady and continual amelioration of the
world.

A brilliant idea!—and of course it could not
be by our author otherwise than brilliantly discussed.   He is so fascinating a writer as to make
one understand, and almost excuse, the senti-
ment—" Errare malo cum Platone quam cum istis
vera sentire."   But after all, truth must prevail
even over eloquence.   He has not proved that
modern negative science involves a religion.   It
never can be proved.   In fact it is easy to demonstrate, *even on his own showing*, that they are
for ever incompatible.   In the next chapter I
shall attempt to prove the inconceivability of a
purely natural religion; and in the two following chapters, to confirm this view by a detailed
examination of the religion which our author
believes himself to have constructed.

CHAPTER I.

IMMORTALITY.

THERE are two kinds of supernaturalism which ought to have been distinguished, but which, as a matter of fact, are persistently confused by our author: the one is synonymous with miracles; the other is not. The word supernatural means, etymologically of course, that which is beyond nature; for when it was invented, men had a notion that the proper dwelling-place of Deity was somewhere just over the firmament, or otherwise beyond the reach of mortal ken. The gods were supposed to haunt

> "The lucid interspace of world and world,
>   Where never creeps a cloud, or moves a wind,
>   Nor ever falls the least white star of snow,
>   Nor ever lowest roll of thunder moans,
>   Nor sound of human sorrow mounts, to mar
>   Their sacred everlasting calm."

But there is, or at any rate there may be, a supernatural *within* nature as well as *without.*

Hercules and Jupiter, *e.g.*, were thought to be no less supernatural when they came down to earth than when they remained at home in Olympus. Or to take more modern illustrations, it is supernaturalism to believe in fate or destiny as an *external* force, interfering with our volitions, preventing us from willing except in certain predetermined ways; it is also supernaturalism to believe in the will itself as an *internal* force, as the faculty of a soul which is spiritual, divine, and immortal. It is supernaturalism to believe that God occasionally interferes with the ordinary course of Nature; it is also supernaturalism to recognise divine meanings and purposes in common objects and events. There is, then, an ordinary and an extraordinary supernaturalism. By extraordinary supernaturalism we are to understand interferences with, departures from, the customary course of things—or in one word, miracles. By ordinary supernaturalism we are to understand supersensible, non-material existences, manifested through the customary course of Nature—viz., a soul within the brain and a God within Nature—or in one word, immortality.[1]

Now it is important to distinguish between these two kinds of supernaturalism, for two rea-

---

[1] I pointed out on p. 4 why the word immortality might be used as a convenient abbreviation to express the reality of God and the soul.

sons. First of all, it is possible to believe in either without believing in both. The Jews imagined that God was constantly interfering with the course of Nature; but, as a rule, they had no faith whatever in a future state. Whereas in modern times, many persons who feel perfectly convinced of their own immortality, would be utterly incredulous in regard to the best-authenticated miracle. Should it be said that immortality is as great a miracle as anything else, I reply— Not so. Miracles are a departure from the ordinary course of Nature; immortality is a continuance of it. If there be a soul,[1] it is something distinct from brain. That is what soul means. And as the brain and the soul are distinct existences during life, there is no violation of the course of Nature if they remain distinct existences after death. So that it is possible to believe in immortality, and at the same time to believe in the absolute unchangeableness of the ordinary course of Nature.

But secondly, it is important to distinguish between the two kinds of supernaturalism, because, though religion is conceivable without the one, it is not, as I shall endeavour to show, conceivable without the other. Miracles form no part of the *essence* of religion. God might have existed, and been recognised as existing, even

---

[1] Some of the reasons which necessitate a belief in a soul or ego, the reader will find in my Essay on Personality.

though He had never once interfered with the
customary order of events. In Mohammedanism,
as our author justly points out, we have an ex-
ample of a religion which exercised a wide, and
in many respects a good, influence, without re-
lying at all upon the evidence of miracles. Even
in Christianity they are at any rate of very
secondary importance.

" Let us imagine" says our author, "all miracles ex-
ploded, and the word 'miracle' itself, except in the sense
of a phenomenon as yet unexplained, dismissed to the
vocabulary of poetry. Would the word 'miracle,' thus
passing out of serious use, carry with it the word 'God
" Who does not call to mind those passages in the New
Testament in which—so strangely to those whose faith
rests on Paley's Evidences—the demand for miracles is
treated with contempt? Such passages show that even
in a scheme of religion in which miracle plays a considerable part it is not regarded as the only mode of divine
action, but rather as the sign of some important change in
the mode of divine action, some new dispensation. They
show that the great founders of Semitic religion worshipped rather the God who habitually maintains His laws
than the God who occasionally suspends them."[1]

True enough! But the writer seems to imagine, because miracles are not essential to religion,
that immortality may be as readily dispensed
with. This appears to me the fundamental
mistake of the book. Instead of giving us a
clear definition as to what he means by super-

[1] P. 81.

naturalism, he uses the term vaguely and hesitatingly—sometimes for miracles, sometimes for immortality, sometimes for both. He makes no attempt to distinguish between ordinary and extraordinary supernaturalism, between a supernatural *without* and a supernatural *within* Nature; between miracles, which are at best but the evidence of a religion, and immortality, which is, as we shall see, its basis. The two subjects cannot properly be discussed together; but our author persists in confusing them. And much of the plausibility which his book possesses is due to the argumentative advantages arising from this ambiguity. For instance, he says :—

"I maintain that the essential nature of religion is popularly misconceived, and that an accident of it—viz., supernaturalism—is mistaken for its essence.[1] . . . There is no necessary connection between theology and supernaturalism."[2]

This is true enough, self-evidently true, in regard to the one kind of supernaturalism; but it is demonstrably false in regard to the other.

Again, he says :—

"In the residuum left after the elimination of miracle we have . . . something which has all the greatness and sublimity of the old religion. Not morality, but worship; . . . a principle of life possessing the whole imagination and heart."[3]

This might be true, if the term miracle were

[1] P. vi, 2d edition.   [2] P. 41.   [3] P. 141.

B

used in its strict and definite sense; but our author means it to include immortality; and if we eliminate that from the universe, worship, as we shall see, becomes an impossibility.

Once more, he says :—

"It was honestly believed that supernatural occurrences had happened and could be authenticated, and that such occurrences were calculated to throw new light upon the relation of God to man. If this belief was a delusion, theology must learn to confine itself to Nature."[1]

But besides supernatural *occurrences*, — viz., miracles,—there are, or at any rate conceivably may be, supernatural *existences*—viz., the soul and God; in other words, there may be supernatural elements within Nature itself. Were miracles for ever disproved, it would not follow that there was nothing in the world but matter : it would still be possible that if we looked deeply enough into Nature, we should find it to be in reality supernatural.

In more than one place, again, our author confuses immortality with " future punishments miraculously announced." But manifestly it is quite possible to believe in a future state, the announcement of which has not been attended with any violation of the course of Nature. Plato was a firm believer in immortality, but no one imagines that he had received any miraculous intimations in regard to it.

[1] P. 67.

We find the same kind of confusion, too, when our author comes to inquire, What is the essential meaning of the word "God"? Is the old theological view, he asks, exhaustive or not?

"Is it all summed up in the three propositions that a Personal Will is the cause of the universe, that that Will is perfectly benevolent, that that Will has sometimes interfered by miracles with the order of the universe ?" [1]

Our author fails to perceive that these propositions do not stand on the same footing. We can conceive of a Deity who never interfered with the uniformity of Nature; but we cannot look upon any being as a God, unless we can regard him as possessing benevolence, and so much of Personality, at least, as benevolence implies.

Curiously enough this is acknowledged by our author in one of those singular contradictions in which the book abounds. In comparing the growth of the modern spirit to the progress of a human being from youth to manhood, he says :—

"Manhood differs from youth, not merely in having recovered something which youth had parted with [viz., cheerfulness], but also in having gained something unknown both to youth and childhood. Beyond the forms of nature and the ideal of moral goodness there remains another discovery to be made, the recognition of a Law in the universe stronger than ourselves and different from ourselves, and refusing to us not only the indulgence of

---

[1] P. 13.

our desires, but also, as we learn slowly and with painful astonishment, the complete realisation of our ideals. It is not in the time when we are forming those ideals that it is possible for us to recognise the limitation imposed by Nature upon the fulfilment of them, and yet until we can make the recognition we shall be liable to constant mistake and disappointment. The special advantage of manhood over youth lies in this recognition, in the sense of reality and limitation. Youth is fantastic and utopian compared to manhood, as it is melancholy compared both to manhood and childhood. . . .

" 'All things are possible to him that believeth,' is a glorious formula of philanthropic heroism ; the mistake of the Church, as the mistake of young men, is to treat it as literally and prosaically true.

"Another maxim has to be learned in time, that some things are impossible, and to master this is to enter upon the manhood of the higher life. But it ought not to be mastered as a mere depressing negation, but rather as a new religion. The law that is independent of us and that conditions all our activity is not to be reluctantly acknowledged, but studied with absorbing delight and awe.

"This assuredly is the transition which the world is now making. It is throwing off at once the melancholy and the unmeasured imaginations of youth ; it is recovering, as manhood does, something of the glee of childhood and adding to that a new sense of reality. Its return to childhood is called *Renaissance*, its acquisition of the sense of reality is called Science. We may be glad of both.

.   .   .   .   .   .

"Nevertheless, the analogy that we have been pursuing will suggest to us that the victory of the modern spirit would be fatal if pressed too far, as indeed it is essentially a melancholy triumph, and that the youth of humanity, crushed out too ruthlessly, would have a still more irresistible Renaissance than its childhood. The sense of reality gives new force when it comes in to correct the vagueness of our ideals ; this is manhood ; but when it takes the place or destroys the charm of them, this is the feebleness of old age. Healthy manhood must continue to savour of its youth as of its infancy, to be enthusiastic and tender as well as to be buoyant. It must continue to hope much and believe much ; we praise caution and coolness in a youth, but a few stages on these qualities cease to seem admirable, and the man begins to be praised for the opposite qualities, for ardour, for enthusiasm—in short, for being still capable of that of which youth is only too capable. But in the individual we regard this persistent vitality as only possible for a time. Old age sets in at last, when, if enthusiasm still survive, it is not so much a merit as a kind of prodigy. Is Humanity to verify the analogy in this respect also ? When we have learnt to recognise the limitations imposed on us, that we cannot have everything as our enthusiasm would make it, and that if our ideals are to be realised in any considerable measure it must be by taking honest account of the conditions of possibility ; when we have gone so far, are we to advance another step and confess that the conditions of possibility are so rigorous that most of our ideals must be given up, and that, in fact, humanity has little to hope or to wish for ? It need not be so, if, as was said above, the service of Necessity may become freedom instead of bondage, if the Power above us which so often checks our impatience and pours contempt on our enthusiasms can be conceived as not necessarily giving less than we hope for because it does not give precisely *what* we hope for, but perhaps even as giving infinitely more. On this hypothesis humanity may preserve the vigour of its manhood. Otherwise, if reality, when we acquire the power of distinguishing it, turns out not merely different from what we expect but much below what we expect ; if this universe, so vast and glorious in itself, proves in relation to the satisfaction of our desires narrow and ill-furnished, if it disappoints not only our particular wishes but the very faculty of wishing by furnishing no sufficient food, then humanity has also its necessary old age. And if its old age, then surely that which lies beyond old age. We must not merely give up the immortality of the individual soul—which some have persuaded themselves they can afford to give up—but we must learn to think of humanity itself as mortal. We must abandon ourselves to pessimism."[1]

According, then, to our author, if we are to escape pessimism, if we are to have a religion and a God, it is necessary that we regard the Power above us as not giving us less than we hope for, but rather as giving us infinitely more. To regard it in this way, I need hardly point out, is to regard it as benevolent and personal; for we cannot conceive of an unbenevolent and impersonal being thwarting us for a time, in order to do in the end "exceeding abundantly above all that we can ask or think." And further, according to the author, if we are to avoid pessimism, if we are to have a religion and a God, it is necessary that we believe in the ultimate realisability of our ideals. Now man finds himself endowed with two ideals, an ideal of happiness and an ideal of perfection, neither of which is ever realised on earth. As to the first—the ideal of happiness—some of us may be scarcely fair judges. We are apt to exaggerate the pleasantness of existence. We have been surrounded

---

[1] Pp. 152 *et seq.*

from our cradles with all the comforts which money could procure. We have scarcely had a wish that was not gratified. We seldom suffer any sort of pain, The prizes of life are, or will be, ours. Kindness and affection are unceasingly lavished upon us. We are more or less accustomed to be petted, caressed, and idolised. Yet, perchance, even we may be doubtful as to whether we can call ourselves happy. At any rate our happiness, if happiness it be, is not the restful satisfaction of our ideal. And we must remember that to immense numbers of our fellow-creatures life is infinitely sad. To many it is a struggle for bare subsistence; a struggle monotonous, uninteresting, disappointing, wearisome. There have been, and are, and will be, a vast multitude to whom the word love is an unmeaning term. Does not your heart ache for that vast procession of the unloved, whose life-path lies through dreary desert wastes, where the flowers of affection never bloom? " Somewhere, somewhere," as Oliver Wendell Holmes passionately remarks, " love is in store for them; the universe must not be allowed to fool them so cruelly." Yes! somewhere there must be compensation for the unsatisfied yearnings of earth. If not, humanity is a contemptible failure, and its Creator is unworthy of the name of God.

Similarly in regard to our ideal of perfection. Some of us, again, may be inclined to underrate the moral difficulties of life. We were carefully nurtured in our childhood; shielded from everything that could degrade, surrounded with everything that would ennoble. We have been highly educated. All the literature of the world, every country of the globe, is within our reach. There is no end to the culture which we may easily acquire. All our associations are such as tend to stimulate the higher faculties, and to develop in us an exalted type of manly Christian character. But we must not forget how many there are at the other end of the scale, whose surroundings from the cradle to the grave are so filthy and degrading that for them in this life moral depravity is an *inevitable necessity.* And for the favourably circumstanced, as for the unfavourably, perfection is quite unattainable on earth. In fact, the more progress we make the more conscious we become of our distance from the goal. Moreover, in striving for the moral welfare of our fellows we are disappointed and discouraged no less than in striving for our own. We accomplish little or nothing; life is so short, and the obstacles to be contended with so great. You remember the touching soliloquy in Tennyson's " Passing of Arthur ":—

" O me ! for why is all around us here
    As if some lesser god had made the world
    And had not force to shape it as he would ?

    .   .   .   .   .   .

Perchance because we see not to the close.
For I, being simple, thought to work His will,
And have but striven with the sword in vain;
And all whereon I leaned, in wife and friend,
Is traitor to my peace, and all my realm
Reels back into the beast and is no more.
My God, Thou hast forgotten me in my death;
Nay, God my Christ, I pass, but shall not die."

Yes; he, and such as he, cannot perish. If death made an end of them for ever, then, I say again, humanity would be a contemptible failure, and its Creator would not deserve the name of God. If we are to escape pessimism and have a religion, it is necessary for us to believe, says our author, " that the Power which checks and thwarts us intends to give us in the end not less than we had hoped for, but rather infinitely more." Is it giving us infinitely more, when we have such a passionate longing for immortality, to answer it by annihilation? Is it giving us infinitely more, when we have yearned and struggled for perfection, to cut us off before it can possibly be achieved? Is it giving us infinitely more, to turn to destruction the whole human race, when so many of them have never tasted the cup of happiness, when so many of them could not but be vile?

If this world be not complete in itself, but only a part of a larger system, if this life be merely a discipline and preparation for a better, then it is conceivable that misery and inequality may be but necessary means to an infinitely glorious end, and that our light affliction, which is but for a moment in comparison with the eternity before us, will work out a far more exceeding weight of glory than could ever otherwise have been ours. But if this world be a system complete in itself—if this life is not to be followed by another—if hopes are born only to be blighted, yearnings roused only to be crushed, beings created only to be destroyed,—then the Author of Nature is either very wicked or very weak. If he had skill he had not love; if he had love he had not skill. Either he does not desire the wellbeing of his creatures or he could not accomplish it. A being like that, is, of course, no object for worship. He deserves only pity or execration—pity if such a world is the best he could make, execration if it is not. God and immortality stand or fall together. Those only can worship who feel in their heart of hearts,

> " Though suns stand still and time be o'er,
> We are, and shall be, evermore."

CHAPTER II.

THE NEW GOD.

RELIGION our author describes as absorbing contemplation— some spiritual object more necessary than livelihood, more precious than fame.[1]

" Without some ardent condition of the feelings religion is not to be conceived, and it has been defined here as habitual and regulated admiration ; if the object of such admiration be unworthy, we have a religion positively bad and false—if it be not the highest object, we have an inadequate religion ; but irreligion consists in the absence of such habitual admiration, and in a state of the feelings not ardent, but cold and torpid." [2]

Such a bad or false religion, he admits, is more properly called superstition.

" In comparing religions in order to discover their common property, it has always been tacitly assumed that there is a species of religion which is noble, and that our concern was with this alone.   But assuredly there is also a species of religion which is bad intrinsically, and yet is of such

---

[1] P. 108.   [2] P. 129.

common occurrence that it might almost lay claim to determine the sense which should be given to the word religion. Religion has been regarded here as the link of feeling which attaches man habitually to something outside himself, and it has been assumed that this feeling is always of the nature of admiration and love. But as a matter of fact, it is quite as often of the nature of terror. If we chose to describe religion as a nightmare eternally troubling man's repose, depressing all his powers with slavish dread and tempting him to terrible crimes under the name of expiations, history no doubt would amply bear us out. But on the whole, in the modern world the better aspect of religion has vindicated itself. The word is now more naturally used in a good sense. It is no longer convertible with superstition. We recognise that men have at times a vision of something mighty and horror-striking which makes them grovel in the dust, and that this is superstition; but that they have also, at other times, a vision of something as glorious as it is mighty, and that this is religion." [1]

Now it is important to bear in mind this distinction of our author's, because if we hold him to it, we shall see that he has only succeeded in constructing a new superstition.

[1] P. 238. He adds what seems to be at first sight a saving clause :—

"Nevertheless, though we can thus distinguish in thought religion from superstition, we cannot always prevent them from being intricately mixed together in fact. It has rarely been found possible to extract from religion the nobler element, so as to escape suffering at the same time from its wasting influence. Not only in Tauris or in Mexico, but here in England, religion has been and is a nightmare, and those who flatter themselves that they have shaken off the horror find a colder, more petrifying incubus, that of Annihilation, settling

Let us now inquire what are the character-istics of the new God, the God of the so-called Natural Religion, who is to excite in us an ardent condition of the feelings ; to keep us in a state of absorbing contemplation ; to be re-garded as more necessary than livelihood, more precious than fame ; to become, in a word, the object of our habitual admiration or worship.

" If, on the one hand, the study of Nature be one part of the study of God, is it not true, on the other, that he who believes only in Nature is a theist, and has a theology ? Men slide easily from the most momentous controversies into the most contemptible logomachies. If we will look at things, and not merely at words, we shall soon see that the scientific man has a theology and a God—a most im-pressive theology, a most awful and glorious God. I say that man believes in a God who feels himself in the pres-ence of a Power which is not himself and is immeasurably above himself—a Power in the contemplation of which he is absorbed, in the knowledge of which he finds safety and happiness. And such now is Nature to the scientific man. I do not now say that it is good or satisfying to worship such a God, but I say that no class of men since the world began have ever more truly believed in a God, or more ardently, or with more conviction, worshipped Him. Com-

---

down upon them in its place, so that one of them cries out, *Oh ! reprends ce Rien, gouffre, et rends-nous Satan.*"

This, however, is only another way of saying that the term "religion" has frequently been applied to what ought to have been called "superstition." The same object cannot possibly be both inspiring and depressing to the same person at the same time, cannot possibly call forth from him simul-taneously both horror and love.

paring their religion in its fresh youth to the present confused forms of Christianity, I think a bystander would say
that though Christianity had in it something far higher
and deeper and more ennobling, yet the average scientific
man worships just at present a more awful, and, as it
were, a greater Deity than the average Christian. In so
many Christians the idea of God has been degraded by
childish and little-minded teaching ; the Eternal and the
Infinite and the All-embracing has been represented as
the head of the clerical interest, as a sort of clergyman, as
a sort of schoolmaster, as a sort of philanthropist. But
the scientific man *knows* Him to be eternal ; in astronomy,
in geology, he becomes familiar with the countless millen-
niums of His lifetime.   The scientific man strains his
mind actually to realise God's infinity. As far off as the
fixed stars he traces Him, 'distance inexpressible by numbers that have name.' Meanwhile, to the theologian, infinity and eternity are very much of empty words when
applied to the object of his worship. He does not realise
them in actual facts and definite computations.

"But it is not merely because he realises a stupendous
Power that I call the scientific man a theist. A true theist
should recognise his Deity as giving him the law to which
his life ought to be conformed. Now here it is that the
resemblance of modern science to theology comes out most
manifestly.   There is no stronger conviction in this age
than the conviction of the scientific man, that all happiness depends upon the knowledge of the laws of Nature,
and the careful adaption of human life to them. . . .
Luther and Calvin were not more jealous of the Church
tradition that had obscured the true word of God in the
Scriptures, than the modern man of science is of the metaphysics and conventional philosophy that have beguiled
men away from Nature and her laws. They want to re-
model all education, all preaching, so that the laws of
Nature may become known to every man, and that every

one may be in a condition to find his happiness in obeying them. They chafe at the notion of men studying anything else. They behave towards those who do not know Nature with the same sort of impatient insolence with which a Christian behaved towards the worshippers of the Emperor or a Mohammedan towards idolaters. As I sympathise very partially with the Mohammedan, and not quite perfectly with the early Christian, so I find the modern scientific zeal sometimes narrow and fanatical ; but I recognise that it is zeal of the same kind as theirs—that, like theirs, it is theological.

"An infinite Power will inspire awe, and an anxious desire to avoid a collision with it. But such awe and fear, it may be said, do not constitute worship ; worship implies admiration, and something which may be called love. Now it is true that the scientific man cannot feel for Nature such love as a pious mind may feel for the God of Christians. The highest love is inspired by love, or by justice and goodness, and of these qualities science as yet discerns little or nothing in Nature. But a very genuine love, though of a lower kind, is felt by the contemplator of Nature. Nature, even if we hesitate to call it good, is infinitely interesting, infinitely beautiful. He who studies it has continually the exquisite pleasure of discerning or half discerning and divining *laws;* regularities glimmer through an appearance of confusion ; analogies between phenomena of a different order suggest themselves and set the imagination in motion; the mind is haunted with the sense of a vast unity not yet discoverable or nameable. There is food for contemplation which never runs short ; you gaze at an object which is always growing clearer, and yet always, in the very act of growing clearer, presenting new mysteries. And this arresting and absorbing spectacle, so fascinating by its variety, is at the same time overwhelming by its greatness ; so that those who have devoted their lives to the contemplation scarcely ever fail to testify to the endless delight it gives them, and also to the overpowering awe with which from time to time it surprises them.

"There is one more feeling which a worshipper should have for his Deity, a sense of personal connection, and, as it were, relationship. The last verse of a hymn of praise is very appropriately this—'For this God is *our* God for ever and ever ; He will be our guide even unto death.' This feeling, too, the worshipper of Nature has. He cannot separate himself from that which he contemplates. Though he has the power of gazing upon it as something outside himself, yet he knows himself to be a part of it. The same laws whose operations he watches in the universe he may study in his own body. Heat and light and gravitation govern himself as they govern plants and heavenly bodies. 'In Him,' may the worshipper of this Deity say with intimate conviction—'in Him we live and move and have our being.' When men whose minds are possessed with a thought like this, and whose lives are devoted to such a contemplation, say,—'As for God, we know nothing of Him ; science knows nothing of Him ; it is a name belonging to an extinct system of philosophy;' I think they are playing with words By what name they call the object of their contemplation is in itself a matter of little importance. Whether they say God, or prefer to say Nature, the important thing is that their minds are filled with the sense of a Power to all appearance infinite and eternal, a Power to which their own being is inseparably connected, in the knowledge of whose ways alone is safety and wellbeing, in the contemplation of which they find a beatific vision." [1]

You will observe, then, that the new God has four characteristics, which, according to our au-

[1] Pp. 19-23.

thor, entitle him to, and insure for him, worship.
First, he is infinitely and eternally powerful.
Secondly, he gives us the law of our life. Thirdly,
he is an interesting study. And fourthly, he is
intimately connected with us.

The first of these characteristics—viz., power
—is the one which is chiefly recognised by modern science, and it is the one on which our author
lays the chief stress :—

> "Atheism may also be called childishness, for the child
> naturally discovers the force within it sooner than the
> resisting necessity outside. Not without a few falls in the
> wrestle with Nature do we learn the limits of our own
> power, and the pitiless immensity of the power that is not
> ours. But there are many who cannot learn this lesson
> even from experience, who forget every defeat they suffer,
> and always refuse to see any power in the universe but
> their own wills."[1]

To be a theist, then—to believe in God, according to him—is to recognise the pitiless immen-
sity of the power that is not ours. Now, surely
a moment's reflection will show the incorrect-
ness of this view. Power alone will no more
make a deity than weight alone will make a man.
There is nothing in the universe less beautiful,
less glorious, less divine, than power *as such*. It
may, no doubt, be possessed by a god, but it may
also be possessed by a fiend. Power ! why, if that
were a test of worth, a successful prize-fighter

[1] P. 28.

C

must be regarded as the most excellent of men.
Power! why, a ton of mud could crush the life
out of the best of us: is that any reason why we
should worship mud? Nor is *infinite* power as
such any more adorable than finite power. Infinity is not divine. It is an attribute of God,
but it is also an attribute of space. Much of
our author's description of the former might be
applied quite as well to the latter. "The mind
is haunted by the sense of a vast unity not yet
discoverable; there is food for contemplation that
never runs short; you gaze on an object which
is ever growing clearer, and yet always in the
act of growing clearer, presenting new mysteries."
Shall we, then, fall down in adoration before the
idea of space, because it is infinite, and therefore
mysterious? So that neither power, nor infinite
power, are in themselves, or for themselves, adorable. In fact power, apart from wisdom and
goodness—and these are precisely the elements
which modern science eliminates from the universe—power *per se* is not beautiful, but terrible.
The greater the power, the more dreadful does it
appear, so that infinite power would be infinitely
terrific. To see only power in Nature, therefore,
is not to find a God. It is "to have a vision of
something mighty and horror-striking," which, as
our author has rightly told us, is superstition.

But secondly, the power is recognised as giving us, in the regularity of its operations, the law

of our life. Here, at any rate, he thinks we shall find a stimulus to worship:—

"Atheism is a disbelief in the *existence* of God—that is, a disbelief in *any* regularity in the universe to which a man must conform under penalties." [1]

Again, he says all beauty, all glory, is but the presence of law; [2] and he argues by implication that the converse follows—viz., that all law is the presence of beauty and glory. Now the term law, in science, only means invariable sequence, customary order of events, the way in which they happen, or in one word—and it is our author's—regularity. He seems to be possessed by the curious delusion that there is something admirable and adorable in mere regularity. As if there were not bad regularities as well as good! Laws, for instance, existed in Thuggee—that remarkable system of garotting which was once so common in India. According to one of these, a Thug was bound to strangle any stranger (with certain specified exceptions) whom chance might throw in his way; and this law was never disobeyed. So that if regularity is to be worshipped, we must worship Thugs. It was wittily said of a very selfish man that he never did a kind action but once, and then he immediately repented of it. Shall we go into raptures over the *law* of that man's life? His

[1] P. 27.　　　　　[2] P. 32.

conduct was regular enough, to be sure, but his sole chance of admiration would have been in occasional irregularities.

Nor is there anything glorious in the mere fact that a law conditions our activities, and that we must conform to it under penalties. The master's will is the slave's law of life, which conditions his activities, and to which he must conform under penalties. But is that any reason why the slave should regard it with habitual admiration or worship, as an object more necessary than livelihood, more precious than fame? What makes a law admirable, if it be admirable, is not the fact that it is a law, but that its results are good; not that it conditions our activities, but that it conditions them beneficially. Now, apart from immortality, which modern science denies, the results of natural law are by no means satisfactory. Apart from immortality, man is a failure, the universe a mistake, and the final result of evolution an anti-climax. The law of the universe, then, on this view of it, is not an object for admiration but for disgust.

But thirdly and fourthly, our author tells us, the power which lays down the law of our life —or in one word, Nature—has two other characteristics which compel us to regard it as a God,—viz., it is an interesting study, and it impresses us with a sense of personal relationship. Now these characteristics are incompatible. Nature might, no doubt, be an interesting study, if we were *not* personally related to her, if we watched her altogether from the outside as disinterested spectators. But according to the teaching of modern science, we are not disinterested spectators. There is no spiritual principle within us, different from, and superior to, Nature. We are but small portions of the material world, worked up for the the moment into individuals, but destined before long to lose our personality. Just as we have been organised — earth *from* earth, dust *from* dust, ashes *from* ashes, so we shall be disorganised — earth *to* earth, dust *to* dust, ashes *to* ashes. And that will be the end of us! On the modern scientific view, then, Nature ceases to be interesting, and becomes appalling. True, we are personally related to her; but our personal relationship means just this, that in a few short years she will destroy us.

Dismissing, then, the third and fourth characteristics of the new God, as it is evident we have a right to do, there only remains for our worship a great Power which must be conformed to under penalties. Our author will have it that this Power is beautiful and glorious. The new scientific theology, he says, though it denies the Deity the attributes of tenderness and justice and benevolence, presents us " more fascinating views than ever of his eternal beauty and glory." But if we take away the attributes of tenderness, justice, and benevolence, from the Power which is not ours, nothing remains but the fact that we must conform to it under penalties—a fact which in itself, as we have seen, is neither beautiful nor glorious.   But, he tells us, " in the knowledge of its ways we find safety and wellbeing." [1]   *Do we?*   Why, to know this Power is to know that we have been created by it, only, in the end, to be annihilated.

Our author has yet another argument why such a Power deserves to be called God.   It strikes me as one of the most curious pieces of reasoning to be found in the whole range of English literature.

" Do the attributes of benevolence, personality, &c., exhaust the idea of God ?   Are they—not merely the most important, the most consoling of His attributes, but—the only ones ?   By denying them, do we cease not merely to be orthodox Christians, but to be theists ?   .   .   .

" God and Nature express notions which are different in an important particular.   But it is evident that these notions are not the opposites that controversy would represent them to be.   On the contrary, they coincide up to a certain point." [2]

In other words, to believe in Nature is to believe in God, because both possess one attribute in common—viz., power.   If there be any value in this mode of reasoning, the logic of the schools has become obsolete, and we require a *norum organon re-renovatum.*   We have always been

[1] P. 23.   [2] P. 17.

accustomed to believe that the *differentia* formed an important part of the definition. Our author thinks it may be altogether omitted. In religion —as distinct from superstition—God has hitherto been regarded as a Power differentiated from other powers by the possession of infinite justice and infinite benevolence. But, argues our author, since power is power, whether just and benevolent or not, since power and God have one attribute in common—viz., strength—therefore they may be used as synonyms. Let me illustrate this by a parallel case. The endowments peculiar to man—such as conscience and language— are not his only attributes; they are but the most important and consoling of his attributes. Man and animal express notions which are different in an important particular, but they are not the opposites which controversy would represent them—they coincide up to a certain point. They both agree in one respect—viz., in the possession of a physical organisation. Animals, therefore, should be called men, and treated with a respect and consideration hitherto denied them!

We see, then, that the God of " Natural Religion " is destitute of all the most essential attributes of Deity. Power he undoubtedly possesses ; but it is exercised unjustly, capriciously, tyrannically, cruelly; for he denies us immortality, without which there can be no compensation for the miseries and inequalities of life. *He ought not, therefore, to be worshipped.*   Our deplorable impotence may tempt us to flatter him; but the language he deserves is the language of contempt.   Though we might never be able to crush him as a Power, we should at all events determine to destroy him as a God.   If we would be really religious, if we would be true to ourselves and to right, we must be prepared, though all the world adored him, to scout him to his face, to say to him as Prometheus said to Jove,—

" Why art thou made a god of, thou poor type
Of anger and revenge and cunning force ?
True power was never born of brutish strength.
Evil hath its errand as well as good ;
When thine is finished, thou art known no more.
There is a higher purity than thou,
And higher purity is greater strength ;
Thy nature is thy doom, at which thy heart
Trembles, behind thick wall of thy might.
He who hurled down monstrous Titan brood
Is weaker than a simple human thought :
Let man but will, and thou art god no more."

CHAPTER III.

THE NEW FAITH.

OUR author has justly told us, as I pointed out in the previous chapter, that while superstition is depressing, religion is essentially inspiring. The object of our habitual contemplation, he says, should make life rich and bright for us.[1] True religion, he observes again, must give the worshipper faith, and faith he defines as confidence that life is not irreconcilably opposed to our ideals.[2] This confidence, he further points out, will become a stimulus to right-doing; the religious being distinguished from the irreligious life by the characteristic of unselfishness.[3] So that, according to our author, the new religion, if it be a true one, must make us (1) happy, or at any rate hopeful, and (2) self-denying. We have now to inquire whether it will stand this test. Can it, or can it not, be called a faith?

In attempting to prove that it can, he makes a

[1] P. 141.   [2] Pp. 61 et seq.   [3] Pp. 235, 236.

most unpromising start—for he tells us that *any*
theory of the universe must be inspiring. In a
single sentence, he uses the expressions—system,
law, way of viewing the universe, and worship
—as synonymous. As if all systems and laws
were necessarily good! As if all ways of viewing the universe must necessarily lead to worship! He seems to forget that there is such a
thing as pessimism, that there have been Schop-
enhauers and Hartmanns. He says :—

"Just as atheism does not consist in a bad theory of
the universe, but in the want of any theory, so theism
consists not in possessing a meritorious or true or consoling
theory, but simply in possessing a theory of the universe.
He who has such a theory acts with confidence and decision; he who has no such theory is paralysed. One of
the rudest of all theories of the universe is that propounded
by Mohammed, yet it raised up a dispersed nation to vigour, union, and empire. Calvinism presents assuredly a
view of the universe which is not in any way consoling,
yet this creed, too, has given vigour and heroism. The
creed of the earliest Romans rested upon no basis which
could for a moment pass for philosophical, yet while it was
believed it gave order to the State, sanction to morality,
victory to the armies." [1]

In regard to these illustrations, I would remark
that Mohammedanism was inspiring not because
it was a theory, but because it was a theory
which gave promise of a future life. That life,
it is true, was not of an exalted character; but

[1] P. 36.

it was quite good enough to make a rude people feel that existence was not irreconcilably opposed to their ideals. To the Romans, it must be admitted, the next world appeared vague and uninviting; but they were taught that *here* at least the services of gods were always to be secured by prayer and sacrifice. This was what gave them confidence. Whoever had discharged *his* part of the bargain was inspired with energy and decision, because he felt assured that the gods would not fail in *theirs.* And as to Calvinism, the belief that the vast majority of the human race will spend their eternity in hell is certainly not in itself a cheerful doctrine. Still the Calvinist, since he is elect—and of course every Calvinist is elect—may look forward hopefully to *his own* future; and from the days of Tertullian until now, there have always been men who could take pleasure in the thought, that the torments of the lost would form a conspicuous feature in the entertainment provided for the saved.[1] So that the theological theories referred to by our author, crude though they were, all contained certain consoling and encouraging ele-

[1] Only a year or two ago, I myself heard a clergyman deliver himself from the pulpit as follows: "My brethren, you may imagine that when you look down from heaven, and see your acquaintances and friends and relations in hell, your happiness will be somewhat marred. But no! You will then be so purified and perfected that, as you gaze on that sea of suffering, it will only increase your joy."

ments. But the modern scientific theory of the universe is *essentially* and *thoroughly* depressing. Essentially and thoroughly, I say; for it leaves no loophole, like the "election" of Calvinism, through which the privileged believer may escape. Modern scientists do not say that unscientific persons will be annihilated, but that *all* will be annihilated, even the scientific theorists themselves. Hence what it behoved the writer to prove was, not that *crude* theories of the universe could be inspiring, but that *depressing* theories could be inspiring. To prove this, however, would be to demonstrate a contradiction.

A second argument of our author's is that there may be inspiration or faith, without any belief in the *benevolence* of the being worshipped.

"It is not the benevolence of his Deity which gives so much energy and confidence to the convinced theist; it is rather the assurance that he has the secret of propitiating his Deity. It was not because Jupiter or Mars were benevolent beings that the Roman went out to battle confiding in their protection. It was because all sacrifices had been performed which the Pontiffs or the Sibylline Books prescribed. Just of the same kind is the theistic vigour which we see in modern science. Science also has its *procuratio prodigiorum*. It does not believe that Nature is benevolent, and yet it has all the confidence of Mohammedans or Crusaders. This is because it believes that it understands the laws of Nature, and that it knows how to act so that Nature shall favour its operations. Not by the Sibylline Books but by experiment, not by supplications but by

scientific precautions and operations, it discovers and pro-
pitiates the mind of its Deity." [1]

But modern science has *not* the secret of propitiating its deity. A knowledge of the laws of
Nature is no doubt useful enough in a certain
limited way. But what of the desire for immortality, which in the present age, as the
writer admits, is singularly strong? The an-
cients, who did not seem particularly anxious to
live for ever, yet believed as a rule in a shadowy
kind of existence beyond the grave. We, to
whom the thought of extinction is appalling, are
explicitly taught by the science of the day that
the tomb leads into the bottomless pit Annihilation. By a very strict observance of natural
laws, we may manage to keep ourselves in existence a few years longer. But that is all.
There our power of propitiation ends. We have
no secret for wringing from the Infinite the one
thing worth having, the one thing which our
hearts most crave, the gift of eternal life.

A third argument, on which our author lays
great stress, is that Nature has had many inspired votaries, and has often received the hom-
age of poetry.[2] Now, with the single exception of
Lucretius, no great poet ever regarded Nature
from the materialistic point of view. And but
for his materialism, Lucretius would have ranked
even higher than he does. "All life and nature,"

1 P. 36.   2 P. 94.

says Professor Sellar, "he thought to be susceptible of a rationalistic explanation. And the greater part of his work is devoted to give this explanation. This large infusion of a prosaic content necessarily detracts from the artistic excellence of the poem." In other words, atoms and molecules, Nature and man regarded merely as so much matter, are not good subjects for poetry.

Our author refers to Goethe and Wordsworth as eminent examples of the inspiring effects of a materialistic Nature. But neither Goethe nor Wordsworth had adopted the modern scientific negations. Both believed in the soul, and God, and immortality. God in Nature, our author himself says, was the object of Goethe's worship. But God in Nature is a very different thing from Nature with all the divine elements carefully eliminated.[1] In Goethe's greatest work, the Earth-spirit says :—

> " In Lebensfluthen, im Thatensturm,
>   Wall' Ich auf und ab,
>   Webe hin und her.
>   Geburt und Grab
>   Ein ewiges Meer,
>   So schaff' Ich am sausenden Webstuhl der Zeit,
>   Und wirke der Gottheit lebendiges Kleid."

[1] P. 97. This kind of confusion occurs again and again throughout the book ; *c.g.*—"It is quite possible to believe in God, and even a Personal God, of whom Nature is the

Nature to Goethe was no mere concourse of atoms, but the garment of life which the Deity wears. What an important part, too, is played by immortality in the same wonderful work! The most beautiful scene in the whole poem is, as it should be, the last, where Faust's spirit, after all its doubts, temptations, conflicts, sins, is —on the intercession of Marguerite and others— finally redeemed. For this exquisite *dénouement* all previous parts of the drama were intended, more or less, to prepare the way. So that if you were to eliminate from 'Faust' the ideas of God, and the soul, and immortality, you would have nothing worth mentioning left.

With Wordsworth, again, the worship of Nature was blended, as our author admits [1] and as everybody knows, with Christian ideas. To Wordsworth, pre-eminently, Nature was supernatural.

Was it not Wordsworth who wrote—

"I have learned
To look on Nature, not as in the hour
Of thoughtless youth. . . . I have felt
A presence that disturbs me with joy

only manifestation." But the two propositions, "There is no God but Nature," and, "God has only manifested Himself in Nature," are totally distinct.

[1] P. 104, where it is mentioned that Wordsworth called the idea of immortality, "the head and mighty paramount of truths."

Of elevated thoughts ; a sense sublime
Of something far more deeply interfused,
Whose dwelling is the light of setting suns,
And the round ocean, and the living air,
And the blue sky, and in the mind of man ;
A motion and a spirit that impels
All thinking things, all objects of all thought,
And rolls through all things " ?

Was it not Wordsworth who wrote—

                              " I have seen
A curious child   .   .   .   applying to his ear
The convolutions of a smooth-lipped shell,
.   .   .   and his countenance soon
Brightened with joy; for murmurings from within
Were heard,   .   .   .   whereby,
To his belief the monitor expressed
Mysterious union with its native sea.
E'en such a shell the universe itself
Is to the ear of Faith ; and there are times,
I doubt not, when to you it doth impart
Authentic tidings of invisible things ;—
Of central peace subsisting at heart
Of endless agitation " ?

Was it not Wordsworth who wrote—

" Our birth is but a sleep and a forgetting,
    The soul that rises with us—our life's star,
  Hath had elsewhere its setting,
    And cometh from afar.
  Not in entire forgetfulness,
  And not in utter nakedness,
But trailing clouds of glory do we come
    From God who is our home " ?

Was it not Wordsworth who wrote—

> " Truths that wake
> To perish never ;
> Which neither listlessness, nor mad endeavour,
> Nor man nor boy,
> Nor all that is at enmity with joy,
> Can utterly abolish or destroy.
>> Hence in a season of calm weather,
>>> Though inland far we be,
>>> Our souls have sight of that immortal sea
>>> Which brought us hither ;
>> Can in a moment travel thither,
> And see the children sport upon the shore,
> And hear the mighty waters rolling evermore " ?

And yet we are asked to accept Wordsworth as an illustration of the enthusiasm that may be developed by a theory of the universe which denies the soul, and God, and immortality. Wordsworth did, no doubt, find a passionate joy in the contemplation of Nature ; but the Nature which he worshipped was *totally different* from the Nature of modern science.

Further, our author justly acknowledges, as I have already mentioned, that a truly religious life must not only inspire us with hopefulness, but must stimulate us to unselfishness. The lower or irreligious life, he says, begins and ends in mere acquisition. It is made up of purely personal cares, and pursues, even in the midst of civilisation, no other objects than those which the savage pursues under simple conditions—self-preservation, personal possession and enjoyment. The higher or religious life is inspired by admiration or devotion. In it men's thoughts are drawn away from their personal interests, and they are made intensely aware of other existences.[1] Now of this higher life, he tells us, the artist and the scientist, as such, afford examples. But he himself admits, in the postscript to which I must presently advert, that the tendency of modern science is *not* in the direction of unselfishness. And what of art?—of that materialistic art which is blind to everything spiritual? Why, instead of inspiring self-denial, it directly fosters selfishness. Read, for instance, what Pater says in the last eloquent chapter of his ' Studies in the Renaissance:' "Every moment some form grows perfect in hand or face; some tone on the hills or sea is choicer than the rest; some mood or passion of intellectual excitement is irresistibly attractive for us, and for that moment only. A counted number of pulses is given us of a variegated life. We are all condemned to die. We have an interval, and then our place knows us no more. Some spend it in listlessness, some in high passions, the wisest in art and song. Our one chance is in getting into this interval as many pulsations as possible." Not a word is here said about self-denial. Pulsations, says Pater—give me pulsations, and let

---

[1] Pp. 147 and 235.

the universe go. Materialistic art, then, on the showing of one of its own exponents, does not even profess to inspire men with unselfishness.

We have now examined briefly, but I trust sufficiently, all the arguments by which the writer seeks to prove that the new religion is inspiring. I proceed to point out that he has himself represented that religion as depressing.

First of all, he gives us the creed of modern science :—

" We have not much reason to believe in any future state. We are content to look at human life as it lies visibly before us. Surveying it so, we find that it is indeed very different from what we could wish it to be. It is full of failures and miseries. Multitudes die without knowing anything that can be called happiness, while almost all know too well what is meant by misery. The pains that men endure are frightfully intense, their enjoyments for the most part moderate. They are seldom aware of happiness while it is present, so very delicate a thing is it. When it is past, they recognise for the first time, or perhaps fancy, that it was present. If we could measure all the happiness there is in the world, we should perhaps be rather pained than gladdened by discovering the amount of it ; if we could measure all the misery, we should be appalled beyond description. When from happiness we pass to the moral ideal, again we find the world disappointing. It is not a sacred place any more than it is a happy place. Vice and crime very frequently prosper in it. Some of the worst of men are objects of enthusiastic admiration and emulation ; some of the best have been hated and persecuted. Much virtue passes away entirely unacknowledged ; much flagrant hypocrisy escapes detection.

"Still, on the whole, we find life worth living. The misery we find ourselves able to forget, or callously live through. It is but not thinking, which is always easy, and we become insensible to whatever evil does not affect ourselves. And though the happiness is not great, the variety is. Life is interesting, if not happy. Moreover, in spite of all the injustice of destiny, all the inequality with which fortune is meted out, yet it may be discerned that, at least in the more fortunate societies, justice is the rule and injustice the exception. There are laws by which definite crimes are punished, there is a force of opinion which reaches vaguer offences and visits even the disposition to vice with a certain penalty. Virtue seldom goes without some reward, however inadequate : if it is not recognised generally or publicly, it finds here and there an admirer, it gathers round it a little circle of love ; when even this is wanting, it often shows a strange power of rewarding itself. On the whole, we are sustained and reconciled to life by a certain feeling of hope, by a belief, resting upon real evidence, that things improve and better themselves around us." [1]

Such a creed, surely, is exceedingly depressing. It does not conform to one of the requirements which our author himself has laid down. It does not make life rich and bright for us. We find in it no object for habitual admiration or worship—nothing that can be contemplated with absorbing delight, as more necessary than live-lihood, more precious than fame. This creed, instead of assuring us that life is *not* irreconcil-ably opposed to our ideals, most forcibly suggests that it *is*. The best it can tell us is, that in the

[1] Pp. 64-66.

more fortunate societies virtue is generally re-
warded, and that things are gradually improving
themselves. But if even one human being has
been *extinguished* without having had fair-play,
if even one human being were used *merely* for
the purpose of bettering his neighbour's circum-
stances, then there is injustice at the heart of
things, and the great Power which is not ours
must be regarded with suspicion and distrust.

Again our author confesses, in so many words,
that the faith of modern science is at best but
superstition :—

"Before Church traditions had been freely tested, there
was one rigid way of thinking about God—one definite
channel through which Divine grace alone could pass—the
channel guarded by the Church He had founded. 'As if
they would confine the Interminable, and tie Him to His
own prescript!' Accordingly, when doubt was thrown
upon the doctrines of the Church, there seemed an immi-
nent danger of atheism ; and we have still the habit of
denoting by this name the denial of that conception of
God which the Church has consecrated. But by the side
of this gradual obscuring of the ecclesiastical view of God,
there has gone on a gradual rediscovery of Him in another
aspect. The total effect of this simultaneous obscuration
of one part of the orb and revelation of the other, has been
to set before us God in an aspect rather Judaic than Christian. We see Him less as an object of love, and more as
an object of terror, mixed with delight. Much indeed has
been lost—it is to be hoped not finally—but something
also has been gained : for the modern views of God, so far
as they go, have a reality—a freshness—that the others
wanted. In orthodox times the name of God was almost

confined to definitely religious writings, or was used as part of a conventional language. But now, either under the name of God, or under that of Nature, or under that of Science, or under that of Law, the conception works freshly and powerfully in a multitude of minds. It is an idea indeed that causes much unhappiness, much depression. Men now reason with God as Job did, or feel crushed before Him as Moses, or wrestle with Him as Jacob, or blaspheme Him ; they do not so easily attain the Christian hope. But with whatever confusion and astonishment, His presence is felt really and not merely asserted in hollow professions ; it inspires poetry much more than in orthodox times. It may be confidently said that in this modern time, when the complaint is so often heard, *ver-storben ist der Herrgott oben*, and after those most recent discoveries which, in the surprise caused by their novelty and vastness, seem to dissipate all ancient faiths at a blow, the conception of God lives with an intensity which it never had before. This very conception indeed it is which now depresses us with its crushing weight. The overwhelming sense of littleness and helplessness of which we complain is not atheism, though atheism has similar symptoms. It is that very thought, ' As for man, his days are as grass,' which is suggested by the contemplation of the Eternal ; it is the prostration caused by a greatness in which we are lost ; it is what we might venture perhaps to call *the superstition of the true God."* [1]

According to this, then, the title of our author's book should have been ' Natural Superstition.' The worship of science will not answer to his description of religion till confidence be added to awe.[2] But confidence, as we have seen,

<hr>

[1] P. 109 *et seq.*   [2] P. 111.

involves immortality, and immortality means supernaturalism. Without supernaturalism, therefore, on his own showing, though there may be superstition, there cannot be religion.

Lastly and specially, I have to point out a remarkable passage in the postscript :—

"When the supernatural does not come in to overwhelm the natural and turn life upside down, when it is admitted that religion deals in the first instance with the natural, then we may well begin to doubt whether the natural can suffice for human life. No sooner do we try to think so than pessimism raises its head. The more our thoughts widen and deepen, as the universe grows upon us and we become accustomed to boundless space and time, the more petrifying is the contrast of our own insignificance, the more contemptible become the pettiness, shortness, and fragility of the individual life. A moral paralysis creeps upon us. For a while we comfort ourself with the notion of self-sacrifice ; we say, What matter if I pass, let me think of others ! But the *other* has become contemptible no less than the self; all human griefs alike seem little worth assuaging, human happiness too paltry at the best to be worth increasing. The whole moral world is reduced to a point ; the spiritual city, 'the goal of all the saints,' dwindles to the 'least of little stars ;' good and evil, right and wrong, become infinitesimal, ephemeral matters; while eternity and infinity remain attributes of that only which is outside the realm of morality. Life becomes more intolerable the more we know and discover, so long as everything widens and deepens except our own duration, and that remains as pitiful as ever. The affections die away in a world where everything great and

enduring is cold ; they die of their own conscious feebleness and bootlessness." [1]

What is this but an eloquent confession that the
modern theory of the universe, so far from being
inspiring, is the most depressing theory with
which ever the world was cursed ?

This brilliant attempt, then, to construct a
natural religion, is a brilliant failure—a failure
because it was an attempt to achieve the impossible.   Without a soul there can be no immortality; without immortality there can be no God ;
without God there can be no worship.   If the
only future to which we can look forward is one
of dissolution and decay, when this earth of ours
will be nothing but

> " A slag, a cinder drifting through the sky,
>   Without its crew of fools ; "

if there must come a time when consciousness
and reason and love shall have for ever passed
out of existence,—then our desire for happiness,
our longing for perfection, our passionate demand
for eternal life, are but ghastly illusions, diaboli-
cal mockeries ; and the great Power which has
implanted them within us deserves not love but
hatred, not honour but contempt.   We can only
worship as we see grounds for believing that our
life in time is a birth into eternity ; that the

[1] P. 261.

sufferings and inequalities of this world are but *preparations* for a happier and nobler state ; that our afflictions, and the afflictions of our brethren, are working out a far more exceeding weight of glory than could ever otherwise have been achieved ; that there is, in a word, a great,

> " Far-off, divine event,
> Towards which the whole creation moves."

THE END.

PRINTED BY WILLIAM BLACKWOOD AND SONS.

THE ORIGIN OF EVIL;

AND OTHER SERMONS.

Second Edition.   Crown 8vo, 5s.

SOME OPINIONS OF THE PRESS.

" The outcome of a powerful and cultured mind. . . . He knows, moreover, how to express his thoughts in clear, vigorous, direct language, pregnant with earnestness and feeling."—*Scotsman.*

" We decidedly recommend them to persons perplexed by the speculations of modern science."—*Spectator.*

" This is a remarkable volume of sermons. Though it consists of only about 300 pages, it contains an amount of thought and learning which might have been expanded into a bulky folio."—*Glasgow Mail.*

" These sermons are some of the very best produced in this country within the last hundred years."—*Inquirer.*

" The author is an original thinker, whose sympathies are very wide." —*Guardian.*

" Mr Momerie is not an ordinary thinker or preacher. His thoughts glow with fire and are fraught with originality. He is evidently a hard student, and one who has taken a wide view of men and things. He is versed in science, and keeps himself abreast of scientific research. His sermons are model sermons in point of literary merit. . . . The second discourse, which treats of the ' Mystery of Suffering,' is a masterpiece for exquisite thought and logical reasoning. There is a cogency, simplicity, and beauty running through each sermon that carries the mind and will of the reader by simple force. We heartily wish that this little volume of sermons could be placed in the hands of every preacher and teacher, whatever their opinions or persuasion."—*Church Union.*

" Die Vorträge zeigen allenthalben eine schöne Harmonie zwischen Schriftwahrheit und Lebenswahrheit."—*Deutsches Litteraturblatt.*

" Der Verfasser behandelt in diesen Vorträgen wichtige Fragen aus dem Gebiet des christlichen Lebens. Wir heben besonders die über das Leiden hervor, in denen der Verfasser tiefe beherzigenswerthe Gedanken ausspricht. Wir nehmen keinen Anstand, diese Vorträge zum Besten zu rechnen, was über diesen Gegenstand gesagt worden."— *Christliches Bücherschatz.*

" The author of the ' Origin of Evil ' will go sadly astray if he does not make his mark on the age."—*London Figaro.*

" We should almost like to have heard these sermons preached. We are willing to read them carefully, and recommend them to others for like reading, even though, in almost every instance, we dissent from the author's pleading."—*National Reformer.*

" These sermons are everything that sermons ought *not* to be."— *English Independent.*

WILLIAM BLACKWOOD & SONS, EDINBURGH AND LONDON.

III.

DEFECTS

OF

MODERN CHRISTIANITY;

AND OTHER SERMONS.

Crown 8vo, 5s.

"Professor Momerie, by his former books, has already laid the foundation of a reputation as a philosophical thinker and an able expositor of religious subjects. The present volume is marked by equal ability, intellectual force, independent and original thinking, and will confirm the favourable opinion which he has already produced. . . . Whatever views readers may detect as different from their own, they will not fail to admire the author's powerful enforcement of the practical side of Christianity. . . . There follows, as the second part of the volume, nine lectures on the Book of Job; and we have not read before, within the same compass, a more masterly and interesting exposition of that great poem. . . . There are also three admirable sermons on 'The Connection between Reason and Faith,' which will repay repeated reading. . . . The volume deserves to be widely read; and whether readers agree or not in all respects with the author, they will not rise from the perusal without feeling that Christianity is something grander than they have ordinarily realised it to be, and that the Christian life is the bravest and most beautiful life possible."
—*Aberdeen Journal.*

WILLIAM BLACKWOOD & SONS, EDINBURGH AND LONDON.

CATALOGUE

OF

MESSRS BLACKWOOD & SONS'

PUBLICATIONS.

www.ingramcontent.com/pod-product-compliance
Lightning Source LLC
Chambersburg PA
CBHW032345020726
47499CB00009B/3174